Angel voices

Angel

Vanessa Lampert

Voices

Hearing the Divine Messages
of the Universe

CICO BOOKS

London

First published in Great Britain by
Cico Books
32 Great Sutton Street
London EC1V 0NB

(020) 7253 7960

10 9 8 7 6 5 4 3 2 1

A CIP catalogue record for this book is available from the British Library

ISBN 1 903116 50 3

Jacket design by Ian Midson
Jacket illustration by Jacqui Mair

Printed and bound in Singapore by Tien Wah Press

Contents

Angels Are All Around Us

The time has come to invite our angels to join and help us
as we strive to make the world a better place.

The word "angel" is derived from the Greek word, angelos, which means "messenger". Angels are the messengers of divine creative energy, but they are also the message itself – their presence alone brings a dimension of spirituality into our lives.

ANGELS AND SPIRIT GUIDES

Angels are celestial beings of pure spirit who dwell in the cosmos and are intermediaries between higher beings and humankind. They have never walked upon the earth, and are beings of light who are always around us. They are androgynous in nature, although many appear in either a male or female form. Archangels (see page 11) have been given familiar male names throughout history.

Spirit guides once lived on Earth and have chosen to return to help the living. They can be called upon to give advice, comfort, and protection. Many spirit guides work specifically with healers. When I channel my spirit guides to allow them to heal through me, I am aware that different guides come through at different times, depending on who I am treating and why. Some recipients of healing tell me that they sense different sets of hands working on them simultaneously.

I know when my spirit guides are working through me because I feel pulsating waves of heat and often a tingling sensation like a mild electrical current. I also find that my hands are guided to a particular area of the body that needs attention. My angels, however, use telepathy, which is enhanced especially when I am writing. An angelic presence gives me a warm feeling of excitement and pleasure.

HOW TO BEGIN

This book aims to help your heart and mind to become receptive to divine communication. My channelled angel messages appear at the end of each chapter to direct your thoughts and lift your personal spiritual energy, helping you to connect with your own angels.

Remember that our angels cannot intercede unless we ask them to. They are happy to respond to calls for protection, love, comfort, and healing, but in return do send your thanks for their constant love and help.

ANGEL MESSAGES

Angels are waiting for an invitation into my life —I just need to ask.

There have never been so many angels awaiting my welcome.

Angelic love and harmony is mine for the asking.

Angels love to communicate. Just tune into their wavelength.

I am one with the power that created me. I invite my angels and guides to nourish me in everything I do.

I know that my angels and guides are waiting to talk to me. I lovingly learn all I need to know so that this can happen.

My darker side cannot be hidden from my angels and guides. They will nourish me with unconditional love while helping me to understand myself better.

I choose to change the way I think and invite my angels to help me to achieve a better life.

I ask my angels and guides to fill this room with the vibration of heavenly love.

I ask that the joy, harmony, and love of angels flows into my life.

I am willing to change the patterns of the way I live and think so that I can become a better and more enlightened person.

CHAPTER ONE

The Angelic Hierarchy

*When someone invites their angels to converse with them, all
the angelic hierarchies rejoice.*

Most of the world's belief systems, including Judaism, Christianity, and Islam embrace celestial beings, the generic term for angels, as part of their cosmologies.

Angels are divided into hierarchical orders, often referred to as spheres or choirs, and there is a diversity of opinion about the membership within each. In the New Testament, celestial beings are divided into seven orders: angels, archangels, principalities, powers, virtues, dominions, and thrones. The Old Testament adds cherubim and seraphim which, together with the other seven orders, comprise the nine choirs of angels in later Christian theology. It is generally agreed that there are three definite orders, with three levels in each. Therefore, "angel" is both a generic term that refers to celestial beings, and a reference to the third level of beings within the angelic hierarchy. In their position within the hierarchy they are closest to us here on earth.

Seraphim is the highest order of celestial beings. Closest to the throne of God, the seraphim sing His praises, chanting "Holy,

Highest level	Seraphim
	Cherubim
	Thrones
Second level	Dominions
	Virtues
	Powers
Third level	Principalities
	Archangels
	Angels

holy, holy" while encircling the throne of God. In Isaiah 6:2, we have a full description of how the seraphim appear, with their four faces and six wings.

Cherubim hold the knowledge of God and are often sent to earth to perform God's tasks. They are the warrior-angels who expelled man from the Garden of Eden, and who guard it to prevent man's return.

Thrones are also known as Ophanim. These angels are the dispensers of God's judgment, acting with impartiality and humility while carrying out His desires. They are described as great wheels covered with a great many eyes and glowing with light.

Dominions are also known as the Hashmallin, and oversee the lower angelic realms. They receive their orders from the seraphim and cherubim and are responsible for ensuring that the cosmos remains in order.

Virtues are concerned with maintaining the aspects of the natural world and also with bestowing blessings upon the material world. These are the angels who make miracles occur. Those who are able to raise their spiritual consciousness connect with the virtues.

Powers act as an elite guard, maintaining the boundary between heaven and earth. They make sure that the souls who leave the mortal world transcend to heaven safely.

Principalities look after and watch the mortal world, guiding and protecting the earth's nations, cities, and towns.

Archangels lead bands of angels and are the messengers of God. There are literally millions of archangels who cover the entire universe, but certain archangels are given the task to look after humanity here on earth. Many are familiar names such as Michael, Gabriel, and Uriel (see pages 11–12).

Angels watch over individual souls, guiding and protecting them. It is angels with whom we aspire to communicate and, if we are lucky, converse with.

The Archangels

I invite the archangels into my life to help me to become
a better and more enlightened person.

The archangels are higher in the angelic hierarchy than the angels. There are millions of archangels in the cosmos, but only a few connect with us here on earth.

GABRIEL: HARMONY, WISDOM, HOPES, AND DREAMS

Gabriel, whose name means "God is my strength," may be our most frequent visitor from the higher realms. This mighty archangel will give you guidance and hope, and help you to focus on your dreams and aspirations. To the followers of Islam, Gabriel is the spirit of truth who dictated the Koran to Mohammed. To the Jews, he is said to be the angel who destroyed Sodom on the orders of God, and who parted the waters of the Red Sea when the Israelites were fleeing the Pharaoh. Gabriel will blow the final horn on the Day of Judgment, at the end of the world. In the New Testament, he appeared to both Mary and her cousin Elizabeth, mother of John the Baptist, to announce the future births of their sons.

MICHAEL: COURAGE, STRENGTH, AND PROTECTION

Michael, whose name is a question, meaning "Who is like God?" – is one of the greatest of all angels. He appeared to Moses in the burning bush, rescued Daniel and his friends from

the lion's den, and forewarned Mary of her approaching death. Michael represents courage and strength in mind, body, and spirit. He is often visualized as wearing a cobalt blue cloak and carrying a sword which is either of metal or a living flame. This sword can cut through cords that bind us to negative emotions and our past (see pages 84–85).

URIEL: PEACE, INSIGHT, AND CLARITY

Uriel's name means "Fire of God". It is said that God sent Uriel to warn Noah of the impending flood. He is the guardian angel of writers, and he will help you to achieve the goals you set yourself. Uriel will also give you the clarity and insight to understand the hidden agendas of others.

METATRON: SELF-ESTEEM AND JUDGMENT

One of the meanings of Uriel's name is "guide", or "measurer". It is said that Metatron was once the prophet, Enoch, who taken by God and transformed into an angel of fire with thirty-six pairs of wings (the only claim for an angel's previous existence in human form). He is mentioned in the Kabbalah (Jewish mystical writings), and he was said to have led the Hebrew tribes through the wilderness. Metatron also stayed the hand of Abraham as he was about to sacrifice his son,

Isaac. He is said to represent divine judgment and to be the overseer of the keepers of the Akashic records, which are thought to be the ethereal memories and thoughts of mankind.

RAPHAEL: HEALING, ABUNDANCE, KNOWLEDGE, AND TRUTH

Raphael's name means "God has healed." Legend has it that Raphael gave a book of Science and Knowledge to Noah to rebuild the world. He is one of the most frequently depicted angels in Western art, painted by Botticelli, Titian, and Rembrandt. Raphael is most associated with healing, on a personal, physical basis and a planetary level. He can assist you in developing your ability for creative visualization. You can use this technique (see pages 19, 35, 51, 53) to call upon him to help generate abundance.

CHAMUEL: LOVE

Chamuel is the angel of love who helps dissolve feelings of low self-esteem. He can guide you toward finding true love in relationships, and help you to express love through creative talents, such as painting and writing. If your heart is broken or bruised, you can call upon Chamuel to help you to mend it. If your heart is blocked through pain or an unforgiving nature, ask Chamuel to help you find forgiveness in your heart.

ANGEL MESSAGES

I call upon the power of the archangels to help light my way to spiritual understanding.

I call upon the archangels because I have begun my spiritual journey and I need help to find my vocation.

I call upon the power of the archangels to surround myself and my family and friends with peace, harmony, understanding, and love.

I call upon the archangels to help me to understand and practice all that they have to teach.

I call upon Gabriel to give me the wisdom that I can be a better person in all my dealings.

I call upon Michael to give me the strength to follow my convictions.

I call upon Uriel to give me insight and clarity in all that I do.

I call upon Metatron to help me to love and approve of myself, and to realize what a special and individual person I am.

I call upon Raphael to help me to seek out knowledge and truth within every situation.

I call upon Chamuel to show me the love in my heart so that I can truly help others.

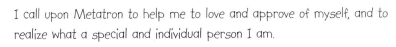

Fallen Angels

I form the light and create darkness. I make peace and create evil. Isaiah 45:7

When we think of fallen angels, we usually think of the dark angels who have rebelled against God and become evil. They are often called names such as the Devil, Satan, Lucifer, Beelzebub, Samael (God's poisoner), and Mephistopheles, amongst others.

The war of attrition of good versus evil, which has been played out since the beginning of time, is in fact the so-called devil acting as an agent of God who has been sent to test the will of man.

The day came when the members of the court of heaven took their places in the presence of the Lord, and Satan was there among them.

The Book of Job 1:6

The reason why evil exists is to give humanity free choice and duality. Without the presence of evil, mankind would always be in a state of purity and goodness, and therefore there would be no virtue in the good that we do. So those often referred to as "fallen angels" are merely serving the will of the creator by constantly testing the darker side of human nature. In fact, we are all part of an experiment whereby we constantly have choices placed before us, and it is up to us to follow the pathway of righteousness so that when we return to God after our sojourn here on earth we are spiritually richer for the experience.

The archangel Lucifer was chosen to oversee the angelic forces who would tempt us from our path of goodness. In order to complete his task successfully, he and his followers agreed to be cast down to hell from where, with great gusto, they tempt us into evil and wrong-doing. However, once this grand experiment is completed, Lucifer and his minions are returned to their true place in heaven.

Once we have been born into our earthly bodies, our memory of our prenatal heritage is forgotten and we have complete free will to choose between positive and negative thoughts and deeds. The battle between good and evil within us is being fought daily; according to the mystical system the Kabbalah, every person has a good and a bad angel hovering above them as they make their choices. Both angels are working very hard at their given tasks.

You may think that you are immune to evil thoughts, but jealousy, anger, ruthlessness, or envy are all a part of the human condition. It is important to cultivate an awareness of this struggle and to be determined to choose angelic light over the darkness.

Guardian Angels

You never walk upon this Earth alone. Your guardian angel is always alongside you, through thick and thin.

Each and every one of us has a personal guardian angel who has been assigned by God to look after and guide us as we spiritually evolve through each of our incarnations or life-times. Our guardian angel is in possession of the blueprint of our lives and spiritual destiny. He will be by your side as you are about to descend to earth for each incarnation, giving you loving support.

After your birth, he will be present always, gently pushing and guiding you along the paths of your destiny, encouraging you to develop spiritually and mature as a balanced, integrated human being. He will help ground you and focus your goals while surrounding you with unconditional love. Your guardian angel will also prompt your conscience to know the difference between right and wrong in your thoughts and deeds.

Your guardian angel is your personal inter-mediary when you wish to talk to the higher realms, conveying your problems or need for guidance. Even when a request is not direct, the response can be intense, as Terry told me.

A WARNING VOICE

Terry Medway, a businessman, told me how a powerful voice in his head warns him whenever he is about to make a bad decision. Although this voice often urges him to take action that appears inappropriate at the time, it always proves absolutely right. He is convinced that this invisible helper is his guardian angel. Terry's guardian angel contacts him in a way that is so powerful that he knows he must take notice, and follow the path along which he is guided.

You will never walk upon this earth alone because your guardian angel will always be alongside you. With many people, however, it is only when they are feeling alone, perhaps in times of great personal crisis, that they become truly aware of the influence of their guardian angels. This cathartic bringing in of angelic help was certainly the case for me.

DARKNESS AND LIGHT

As a child, encouraged by my father who was a healer and Kabbalist, I had an inherited knowledge of many spiritual disciplines including healing, clairvoyance, and channeling. As I grew up, I always wondered how I would use this knowledge for the betterment of mankind. My guardian angel would whisper to me that I would know in time, but not to rush things. In my forties, my guardian told me that the time had come for me to pass on my knowledge. I was shown that I would write a series of books, and that people would come to me from far and wide for healing. But I was also told that the reason I had had to wait for this part of my life to begin was that first I had to learn about life itself.

I married at 22 and had three beautiful and talented daughters. We had a comfortable lifestyle and my husband worked all hours to build up a successful business. Suddenly, in 1996, with two hours' warning, the bank closed down our business and pursued our personal assets. Because my husband decided to fight their decision, they ruthlessly sought to evict us from our home. We had gone from success and security to zero in a matter of hours. Yet from that moment on, my guardian angel was with me more powerfully than ever.

This period that I was going through is often referred to as "the dark night of the soul", meaning that one has to go through times of great despair and pain in order to evolve into thinking and living a more fulfilling life. As with many who experience traumas such as these, it can be a very lonely time, no matter how much you share the problems and stress.

It was during this time that I became very aware of my guardian angel, who comforted me at night when I lay awake, aware of every beat of my heart. On occasions I could even feel his downy wings wrapped around me.

Now, a few years on, we have re-established our equilibrium and have two new successful businesses. I know that my guardian angel made me realize I had to suffer in order to understand life, to become a better person in order to teach and relate to others.

To communicate more fully with your guardian angel, it is wonderful to be able to find out his name.

MEDITATION TO ASK THE NAME OF YOUR GUARDIAN ANGEL

1. Take yourself to a quiet place or your sacred space (see page 49). Sit comfortably, remove your shoes, and place the soles of your feet flat on the floor.

2. Begin to concentrate on your breathing, inhaling deeply and then exhaling.

3. When you are ready, imagine that there are roots growing from the soles of your feet which are penetrating deep into the earth below (no matter how many floors up you are!).

4. Feel the energy from the earth being drawn up into your body through these roots into your feet, legs, and torso, through to your fingers and then up through your throat and to the crown of your head and beyond.

5. Now visualize that the energy flowing from you through the crown of your head is a white light which forms a channel for your guardian angel's easy communication.

6. Invoke your guardian angel and ask him his name.

7. Ask him to help you focus on the angels who are surrounding you to help you to understand and develop your communication with them.

8. Visualize that you are opening your mind and body like a flower to hear your guardian angel's name. Feel yourself filled with the power to hear and understand.

9. When you are ready, go back to concentrating on your breathing and close down the energy flowing through the crown of your head. Visualize the energy of the earth flowing back down through your body, and back down through the roots in the soles of your feet.

10. Thank your guardian angel and the other angels.

11. Open your eyes.

Synchronicity will verify that you have received your guardian angel's name correctly; you will find that you come across it by chance – on a radio or television program, at random in a book, or someone will simply speak it to you out of the blue.

You can also ask to be told the name of your guardian angel in a dream (see dream questions, page 56).

CHAPTER TWO

When Angels Enter Our Lives

Your angels have been waiting patiently for you. Now is the time to welcome them into your life.

Angels love to communicate with us, but the circumstances have to be right in order for us to be able to be aware of their presence. When the timing is right, they will make their presence known.

Most of you reading this book may be already moving toward your spiritual evolvement. There comes a time in many of our lives when we want more than just personal gratification, and embark upon a quest for a more profound set of values – and a life that amounts to more than earning a good wage, having possessions, and entertaining ourselves. We begin to look within for fulfillment and a richer understanding of our spirituality.

Many of you may have begun to seek out spiritual leaders and teachers, through reading or attending workshops, or perhaps by going on pilgrimage to see world-renowned gurus and healers such as Mother Meera in Germany, Sai Baba in India or Buddhist lamas. For each and every one of us our spiritual journey will be unique. You will find that people enter your life at certain times, teach you something, and then depart. Remember that everything happens for a reason.

When you are ready, you can invite angels to communicate with you as part of your natural spiritual development. However, although angels love to be able to enter our lives, because we have free will it is usually up to us to invite them.

Many people go through a period which many call "the dark night of the soul" (see page 18). This journey can be very lonely and painful; often, you do not realize that you have encountered it until it subsides. Part of this experience is to make us understand that much of what we are attached to in the material world prevents us from reaching for, and attaining, a connection with our inner selves and our true vocation. When we have been through traumatic and turbulent times, we emerge with a totally different attitude and as a stronger person. It is often necessary to go through this life-changing stage so that we can turn darkness into light and use the experience for self-healing and self-renewal.

Out of the Blue

One of the most common ways in which angels appear to us "out of the blue" is often in the guise of human strangers who appear in times of distress as if from nowhere. A lady I met told me this story about two friends of hers who were saved by angelic intervention.

ISLAND RESCUE

Thomas and Si had rented a holiday home, a farmhouse on the Greek Island of Corfu. Located at the end of a deserted clifftop path, the friends decided to hire two mopeds in order to explore the island. Returning to the farmhouse one night after dark, Si's moped lurched from the path toward the steep embankment that lead to the cliffside and water below. After frantic searching with no light to guide him, Thomas found Si laying injured.

Although they were miles from the nearest house, a stranger appeared at Thomas' side. He immediately helped Si to his feet – incredibly, the pain from the injury abated and he was able to sit astride his moped. As he turned to the thank the stranger, he disappeared into the night. The friends were convinced that the stranger was an angel, who had simply appeared when they needed him before vanishing when his work was done.

There are many instances of angels appearing out of the blue, lending a helping hand and, when we go to thank them, they disappear almost instantly. Often, it is only on their vanishing that we register that we may have experienced the kindness of an angel rather than that of an ordinary good Samaritan. This is Annie's experience.

AN ANGELIC RECOVERY

Annie and her friends were traveling to a seaside town to perform at an arts centre that afternoon. As members of a conga band, their car was laden with drums and other musical instruments ready for the concert. About half-way through the journey, without warning, one of their tyres blew. The occupants were uninjured but were left stranded – on a quiet road outside a small market town. They had less than one hour to reach their venue, but when Annie looked for the spare tyre in the trunk, it simply was not there. None of the band had cell phones, so they set out to summon help. It began to rain heavily, and the group were wet through; the only visible dwelling was a run-down house in the distance.

Then a youngish woman approached the group, offering to drive them in her jeep to the nearest town. She drove them, eventually, to three towns in order to find the right tyre, then back to their abandoned car. Unbelievably, she even had the correct tools that they needed in order to change and fit the new tyre. As soon as this was done, she said casually, "Bye, then," and drove off before anyone had an opportunity to say anything. They had wanted to offer her thanks and perhaps some money for driving them all over the countryside for over an hour.

Even the rain turned out to be amazing good luck. When the band finally reached their venue, their lateness did not matter, as they discovered that the first part of their concert, which was to have been outdoors, had been rained off. The conga band had nothing

more to do on arrival than enjoy a drink at the local bar before their next performance and talk about their uncanny rescue. From that day, everyone thought of the lady in the jeep as their guardian angel – she even looked angelic with her golden hair – and it seemed strange that she had found them when they needed her, and without them having to ask.

Angels can also throw a powerful shield of protection around you and, if necessary, literally push you out of the way of danger.

Some years ago, I remember walking in the West End of London by an office block that was under scaffolding. I was thrown violently away from the building – and off my chosen path – by my invisible guardian angel. Within seconds, a large metal clip that had secured the top part of the scaffolding fell right in front of me. Had I continued walking, I would have been killed or seriously injured.

When angels are protecting you from danger, it is not unusual for people to find themselves suddenly transported miles within minutes. Chrissy told me this story.

ANGEL IN A TAXI CAB

My train into the city had been delayed by half an hour, which meant that I was running incredibly late for a business meeting. I was feeling anxious enough as I dashed from the train into the main concourse of the station to try to hail a taxi, but I became aware of an eerie silence throughout the station. All I could hear were my own footsteps and the sound of my breathing as I realized that it was

ANGEL MESSAGES

You can feel the love of your guardian angel in all of your actions and deeds.

The name of your guardian angel will come to you in many ways. Remember, there is no such thing as coincidence.

Your guardian angel will always love you unconditionally.

You are never alone. Your guardian angel is always at your side and will never leave it – not even for one second!

From the moment of your birth until the time that you return to the Light, your guardian angel will be guiding, protecting, and loving you.

For all of eternity, your guardian angel is your shadow – always alongside you, but only visible when the right time comes.

Your guardian angel will keep you powerful, safe, and secure.

Your guardian angel will only create loving and harmonious communication. He will keep you safe and well.

Love and approve of yourself. Your guardian angel does!

When you have been through the darkness of despair, you will emerge into the light with a new knowledge and a greater understanding of everything around you.

practically deserted. Outside the station, I spotted a police cordon and I ran up to an officer to ask him what was happening. Strangely, he didn't seem to quite take in what I was asking him and he told me to get out of the area immediately.

I turned and saw a black cab with its light on. The driver smiled, and waited for me to get in before speeding off from the station. I remember looking at my watch; it was 9.00am. I talked on my cell phone as the cab made its way to north London, eight miles through heavy traffic. I knew the journey would take at least forty minutes.

The cab pulled up at my destination, and I got out to pay the driver. As I took my purse from my handbag, he gazed at me and said, "It's nothing", before disappearing. I could hardly believe it. I entered the building and checked my watch: it was 9.15am, which would have been impossible. I asked the receptionist the time and she confirmed it. I later discovered that just four minutes after I had got into the taxi, a large bomb had exploded in the vicinity of the train station.

To this day, I know the taxi driver was my guardian angel, whisking me away from danger. It was an amazing experience that I will never forget.

Answering a Cry For Help

I am sure that for many of you there have been times when you have cried out to your angels and guides for help. These are the times when you are in deepest despair and with little energy to help yourself. This cry often comes directly from your soul. Although your guardian angel cannot change the blueprint of your karma and the lessons and experiences which are contained therein, he will do his utmost to soothe your struggle.

A HOPE AND A PRAYER

Linda's son was taken seriously ill and he was rushed into intensive care in hospital. Linda and her husband were called into their son's room by a doctor, where they were told that things were very serious as their son's bodily functions were shutting down one by one. There seemed to be little that anyone could do to save him.

Linda distinctly remembers her despair as she left her son's bedside to retreat to the bathroom where she could be alone. Behind the closed door, she cried desperately to her angels for their help.

Within minutes, the doctors called her and her husband back into their son's room as he had suddenly – and for no apparent reason – begun to recover. To this day, Linda attributes this miraculous development to the intervention of angels.

Many people find that when they have lived through a terrible experience, such as the loss of someone close or a serious illness, angels offer their love and compassion at very close quarters. They may not be able to prevent you from suffering a great loss, but they can give you comfort in unexpected ways, as the following experience reveals.

A DREAM AFTER DEATH

Even though it happened in a dream, I have always felt that an angel did something wonderful for me. My 12-year-old grandson had died suddenly in an accident. The grief was unbearable. The scene that played over and over in my mind was the very last time I saw him.

His 14-year-old sister had spent the night with me. I had just driven her back home and was backing out of the driveway when I saw my grandson in their yard, and we waved and smiled to each other. Of course, I didn't know that I would never see him again or I would have taken the time to give him a big hug. Three days later, he was gone.

After several weeks of agonizing grief, I dreamed about an angel bringing him down from heaven in her arms. It was an awesome scene; I can't possibly describe it. My grandson and I gave each other a wonderful hug then, just as suddenly as the angel had descended, she returned to heaven with my grandson. I know it was a dream, but it helped me through my grief more than any other thing. It was the most realistic dream I have ever had. Even though it has now been 14 years since the dream, it is still very vivid in my mind.

HOW TO ASK YOUR ANGELS FOR HELP

On a day-to-day basis, your angels will try to guide and assist you if and when you ask for help. You will find that you experience amazing results. Follow the meditation below, ensuring that you are fully relaxed before making your request to your angels.

1. Take yourself to a quiet place or your designated 'sacred space' (see page 49) where you will not be disturbed.

2. Concentrate on your breathing until you are feeling really relaxed.

3. Sense within yourself that you would like to be an open channel with the angelic realms by inviting in your angelic helpers.

4. Feel their energy begin to surround you first, and then permeate through your body.

5. When you feel the time is right, ask them for help with your problems. Be aware of your cry for help coming from the depth of your very being.

6. Concentrate on your request.

7. When you feel ready to move on, concentrate on your breathing again as you feel the angelic energies dissolve from your environment.

8. When you are ready, thank the angels and open your eyes.

When Your Time is Not Up

We are here on Earth to learn lessons to help our souls evolve along their spiritual pathway. Our guardian angel (see page 16) is alongside us, nudging us along our pre-chosen path.

However, as we are human and we have free choice, we sometimes wander inadvertently away from our destiny. This can lead us to a situation where we are in danger of dying before our pre-allotted time, so our angels have to work overtime to try to make themselves heard in order to save us from mortal danger. This is what happened when angels physically interceded in my mother's life, and in turn my life.

GUARDIAN ON A TRAIN

During 1941 when the German Luftwaffe was regularly bombing London, my mother was traveling home from work on the London Underground. The flat that she was living in was almost opposite Warren Street Tube Station, in central London.

However, on that particular occasion she missed her stop at Warren Street Station and found herself at the next station, Goodge Street, which is about two minutes away. As the train slowed down and it pulled into the station, she was aware of a bomb blast in the vicinity.

Warren Street Tube Station had suffered a direct hit, killing everyone who had disembarked from the train that my mother had been on. If she had not missed her normal station, she would have been killed instantly. My father, who was at that time an Air Raid Warden, knew that my mother was due on that train and heard the bomb go off. He rushed over to the disaster area to look for her.

To this day, my mother is convinced that it was her guardian angel who had protected her. There had been no conceivable reason as to why she had missed her normal station, as this was something that she had never done before, and it never happened since. It seemed as if one minute she was aware of approaching Warren Street Station and was thinking about alighting, and the very next moment she realized that she had missed the station and was nearly at Goodge Street. It was as if time had just moved on without her being aware of it.

My father always taught me that time is an extension, as well as an expression, of the mind. If you pick up a book you can open up the pages at the beginning, the middle, and the end; so it is with our lives. Although we are aware of living in the present, our future and its impact on humanity is already set along the timeline of the world.

Suzanne Dawson's two life-saving experiences during childhood convinced her that her angels interceded to stop her dying before her time. Here are her stories.

AN ANGELIC LIFEGUARD

When I was about four years old, I was with my family on holiday in Benidorm, Spain. My mother was looking after me by the hotel swimming pool as my father had taken my older brother out. My mother related to me how, as she momentarily dozed in the hot sun, I made my way toward the swimming pool... and ended up at the bottom. My mother awoke to the clamor of people's distress on witnessing the accident, and as my mother is unable to swim, she began to panic.

My mother recalls that a man with a dog appeared, fully clothed in a hat and coat which I guess must have been a rather odd sight on a hot Spanish summer's day around a hotel pool. He jumped in fully clothed and rescued me. Dripping wet, he then handed me back to my mother and without saying a word simply walked away, vanishing into what would seem thin air. Upon returning, my father and brother tried very hard to find this man, which proved impossible.

Suzanne's next experience is also around water. Again, her guardian angel rescued her, although these memories have caused her to be afraid of water as an adult.

AN ANGELIC RETURN

I was around five or six years old and I was with my family and their friends on a holiday in Britain. I remember playing with my brother and some other children in a man-made shallow enclosure for children along the sea front. All I remember is playing, wading, paddling, and then being alone, away from the other children. The tide must have come in and instead of being in the safe shallow water of the enclosure, I was further away from the beach and standing on the enclosure wall. I could see people on the shore but I was distressed and crying because I felt trapped, unable to get back to safety.

I know that this will sound unbelievable, but I definitely remember that a man just appeared from beneath the water on the other side of the enclosure wall. He put me on his back and swam with me back to the shore and then vanished. When I was reunited with my mother I was very distressed, and told her of this man who had appeared from nowhere, but she said that she had not seen him. I know in my heart that his man had been my guardian angel, who had saved me from drowning.

At Times of Illness

During times of illness, our angels are working overtime to help us to recover. Children, especially, may recall an angel at their bedside, although in retrospect this has been interpreted as a symptom of their illness rather than a reality. Equally, angels appearing near the dying may symbolize the passing on of the soul. Whatever the circumstance, angels do appear to guide a person back to health, or to shepherd their soul onward, depending on a person's destiny. In the following story, my father's guardian angel brought with him the spirit of a family member, who at that time was unknown to him, and who physically performed hands-on healing. Here is my account of his recovery.

A DIVINE DOCTOR

When my father was young, he was very seriously ill with sunstroke. As he lay in a darkened room he saw a vision of a beautiful white glowing angel at the bottom of his bed. His angel smiled at him, then a man appeared and came over to him as he lay on the bed and massaged him with some ointment. Both the angel and the man vanished. Somehow, by the evening my father had made a near recovery and when his mother seemed surprised, he told her that an angel had appeared and brought with him a man who had massaged his limbs and made him better. When questioned, he described the man, and his mother looked shocked as she told him that he had described her father, who had passed away many years before my father had been born.

MEDITATION TO ASK ANGELS TO HELP WITH HEALING

1. Sit or lie down comfortably.
2. Concentrate on your breathing. Inhale deeply, and then exhale.
3. When you feel truly relaxed, sense the presence of your angels.
4. As you inhale, visualize that you are breathing in a white light of pure energy which filters through every part of your body.
5. As you exhale, visualize that you are clearing out any blockages within you.
6. Now ask your angels to fill you with their healing energies. If there is something in particular that you need healed, now is the time to ask.
7. Keep breathing, and feel your angels working on you.
8. If there is someone whom you would like your angels to help, picture that person now and visualize your angels healing them.
9. Visualize your angels working with the white light of their energy and showering that person with their love and care.
10. When you are ready, concentrate on your breathing again and allow the white light of pure energy to leave your body.
11. Thank your angels for all that you have received and for their help. Open your eyes.

You can also ask your angels to help others in the following ways:
1. When you pass a hospital, ask your angels to help those inside recover. By directly asking your angels to intervene, you allow them to be more effective in using their healing energies.
2. Animals can also be helped by angels. Visualize the animal in question, and ask your angels to help speed the animal's recovery.
3. If a person dies suddenly, sometimes their souls can feel very lost and do not immediately rise up to the Source (heaven). Take a moment and ask your angels to help lead these lost souls to heaven so that they can be at rest.

Angels and Medications

You can ask your angels to "charge", or energize any kind of medication including vitamins, minerals, or herbs, in order to help with healing. Hold whatever medication you are taking and invoke your angels. Visualize that they are pouring healing and energizing light into the contents so that they will combine harmoniously with your body.

WHEN BAD NEWS STRIKES

We can feel enveloped by bad tidings from the media on a daily basis. The next time that you read, see or hear bad tidings, take a moment to ask your angels to send some of their healing light and energy to the area. The fact that you are sending out this message helps build an invisible bridge of light and energy along which the angels can direct their energies.

This can be done in the following circumstances.

1. Areas of catastrophe – either natural or caused. Ask your angels to protect, heal, and love those who are involved. Where sudden death has occurred, ask your angels to help those who have suddenly and unexpectedly died to "find the light" as quickly as possible.

2. War zones – do not focus on the terrible things that are happening there, but picture angelic light and energy penetrating every part of the area and its surroundings.

3. Ask your angels to send love and light to the perpetrators of evil who abuse the rights of others.

How Angels Help Us Through Other People

One of the most common ways in which angels help us is through other people. It is amazing how, when you have a problem, strangers come to your aid, give you a message, or have just appeared at the right time from nowhere. Such random acts of kindness are inspired by angels. A friend of mine, Angela Stone, came rushing in to see me as I was writing this book to tell me the following story about her beautiful black labrador, Abraham.

ANGELA'S STORY

A friend of a friend, who lives in the country, rang me out of the blue a couple of days ago. Sadly, her dog had been put to sleep as he had been very ill with arthritis. She had been giving him a herbal remedy and, as she had quite a lot left, she felt that perhaps I would like to have the rest of the bottle for Abraham. I did not know this person but she told me that as she would be in town, she would deliver it to me. I was happy to accept it, although I thought that I would never use it.

That was two days ago, and last night Abraham suddenly could not walk and his limbs were very still. Being a Saturday evening, it was impossible to contact my local vet and I suddenly remembered the medicine in my cupboard. I read the instructions and fed him a dose of the liquid. Together with Charles, my husband, we carried the heavy labrador upstairs to his basket where he slept, as we feared the worst. He was so still that every few hours either I or Charles would check on him to make sure that he was still breathing.

When I woke up the next morning, I could not believe it. Although he was still laying in his basket his nose was wet and damp, and his eyes were bright. He slowly picked himself up, walked around the room and came downstairs. I am sure that somehow my angels had connected with the stranger who delivered the medicine just at the right time.

ANGEL MESSAGES

 When the time is right, your angels will always make themselves known to you.

 Send out angelic love to the world around you and you can make it a better place.

 Your angels like to be invited not only to your celebrations but also to help you overcome life's adversities.

  Obstacles are purposefully placed along our paths so that our angels can help us from stumbling.

 Random acts of human kindness are inspired by angels.

 Lighten up and open up - let your angels brighten up your world and make it a happier place for you.

  Many people act like angels when they reach out a helping hand to support and guide you during your darkest hours. Make sure that you learn from these experiences so that you are there for others.

Our angels try to help save us from ourselves – choose to love life and be open to receiving angelic love and heavenly peace.

 Life is perpetual and can be filled with joy, but it is up to you to live it this way.

CHAPTER THREE

Opening Up to Direct Communication

Your angels have been waiting a long time for you to reach this point in time. Don't keep them waiting any longer!

You will know intuitively when the time is right for you to communicate with your angels. They have been waiting for you to reach this stage in your spiritual development, when you are wanting and hoping for some heavenly communication. Many of you may be aware of the existence of your angels already, so it will come as no surprise when they start to communicate with you.

Caroline is a gifted medium, clairvoyant, and astrologer. She tells me that of every three hundred people who come to her for psychic counselling, she sees an angel at the shoulder of one or two of them. Whenever she mentions this to her clients, they are never, ever surprised. It is merely a confirmation of what they intuitively know.

In order for you to channel angels, it is important that you prepare yourself mentally first. You need to create an open, direct line between you and your angels. To do this, you must start using a part of your mind that you are not physically aware of. Think of manually tuning a radio to a new frequency – this is what you are going to do with your mind, raising your frequency to change levels of awareness to tune into the spiritual, angelic realms.

Your aim is to become a clear and open channel, so that the angels can easily communicate with you and in turn you can receive their energies and presence. To assist you in this spiritual transformation, I have developed six steps to help you achieve communication with the angelic dimensions.

STEP ONE: feel good about yourself

The very first step to opening yourself up to angelic communication is to feel good about yourself by boosting your self-esteem.

Consider that you may feel unworthy of communication at this level. Remember, you are one of God's creations and you were put on this Earth to grow and develop personally and spiritually. Look within yourself and appreciate yourself for who and what you are. Beauty comes from within you.

Take some time to contemplate that this is your life, and you must live it how you see fit. As you grow, so you gather knowledge and a greater understanding of yourself and humanity in general. Realize that you have reached a point where you are seeking something more than just satisfaction and happiness on a physical level.

You may feel guilty about something that is in your past or your present, but you can take steps to free yourself from this. Take a look at what you think you are guilty of and write this down, if it helps. Then make a conscious decision to forgive yourself. For some people, their only fault may be self-punishment through misplaced guilt, which has simply become a habit. There is empowerment through forgiveness, and once you have accepted your genuine faults you can heal the past and move on with your life.

REMEMBER:
You are a terrific person and a testament to the miracle of creation.
Every moment of your life should be fresh and exciting.
There is a spiritual energy within us all; tap into it whenever you need an extra supply of strength and positivity – open yourself up and feel it. Grow and use it.

AFFIRM:
I release the past and joyously look forward to the present.
I have learned from my mistakes, and this knowledge makes me a better person.
I am surrounded by love, and feel secure in its presence.
I release any anger within, and I love and appreciate myself.

STEP TWO: intent

Only you will know if you truly feel comfortable with angelic communication. If you are unsure, visualize that you have already achieved communication with the angelic realms and imagine how you would feel. If you are not completely happy with this, then delay this step until you are more confident about your feelings.

REMEMBER:
Your intention must not be for purely selfish reasons, such as helping you win money.
You must really want communication, and should feel ready for it.

AFFIRM:
This is what I really want. I have been waiting a lifetime for this to happen.
I am ready to open up my heart to angelic love.
I am lovingly and joyously ready to converse with my angels.
I am beyond wondering and now I am wanting. I want my angels to enter my life.

STEP 3: purpose

Make sure that you understand why you want to allow angels into your life. Define your purpose to yourself. Remember that the angels cannot interfere with the blueprint of your life, and neither can they save you from any wrongdoing that you have perpetrated.

Your angels are waiting for you to ask for their help and guidance, but your intentions must be honorable. They cannot help you if the principal aim of your contact is to save you from the outcome of your own stupidity and desires.

Your experience in this lifetime is all a part of your karma, your spiritual growth. You must learn from your mistakes and grow with them. However, once you have learned the appropriate lessons you then can ask your angels to help ease and diminish the pain that you may be suffering, and guide you toward a better and more fulfilled life.

REMEMBER:

Your communication must come from deep within your heart and your soul.

You desire must be honorable.

You place your trust in your angels.

You are determined to grow and develop spiritually.

AFFIRM:

I open up my heart for it to be filled with the purity and light of the angelic realms.

I am treading the pathway of my life but I will now tread it softly and carefully, aware of all of its pitfalls.

I will make my decisions fully aware of the purpose of my life.

I place my trust in my angels to fill me with their love, joy, and harmony, and look forward to it with all my heart.

STEP FOUR: focus

Now you have decided to focus your intention, you will need to work on ways to open yourself up as a spiritual channel through which the angels can contact you. Clear your mind of chaos, otherwise when the messages come they may be distorted.

There are many ways to do this. Meditation is one of the most helpful ways, but there are also other methods. I like to sit in quiet and stillness while others may prefer to clear their mind while walking, using an exercise bike or engaging in any activity in which they find pleasure and are able to focus fully on the present.

The main purpose of this step is to work on your commitment to communication. To begin with, you may sense varying forms of energy around you and flowing through your body. It may take a while for you to become truly aware that these are angelic energies. In order for you to be receptive to the presence of angels, your own spiritual vibrational levels have to be raised. Like tuning the strings of a new violin, the angels will work with you to achieve this so that you are in total harmony with them. When your spiritual vibrational levels have been lifted, the energies will begin to flow with no impediment.

REMEMBER:
Relax; become peaceful and centered.
Become aware of raising your consciousness to new and unexplored levels.
Allow yourself to become an open channel to the spiritual and angelic realms.
Think about your angels frequently, and invite them into your life.
Do not try to apply logic to how you feel. Use your intuition and go with it.

AFFIRM:
I am a clear and open channel with my angels.
My angels have always listened to me – the time has come for me to also hear them.
I have learned how to reach into my soul to experience raised spiritual consciousness.
I am free of congestion and influence. Cosmic energy can flow freely through me.

STEP FIVE: communication

Now that you have taken the previous four steps, you are ready to have a two-way discourse with your angels. You need to activate your intent by finding the best and easiest way to open yourself up to talking with your angels.

I suggest that you use one of the following methods, all of which are explained throughout this chapter – meditation (see page 53), using affirmation cards (see page 54), and dream questions (see page 56). Equally, you can just be still and simply ask.

REMEMBER:
Your angels have been waiting a long time for you to reach this level of spiritual development. They are ready and eager to converse with you.
Relax. When the time is right, it will happen.

AFFIRM:
I feel my guardian angel's wings embrace me.
I am surrounded by the joy, love, and harmony of angels.
I will never feel alone again. I know that my angels love me for who I am, not what I am.
I am grateful that this moment has come, and I look forward to my future life.

STEP SIX: gratitude

Always remember to thank your angels for answering your call. They have given you their unconditional love and protection, so remember to send them your love and thanks in return. Even if you have not yet sensed or seen your angels, once you open up your heart and acknowledge their presence you soon will!

REMEMBER:
Thank your angels for always being alongside you and for answering your call.
Thank your angels for their guidance and constant presence.
Thank your angels for giving you their unconditional love.

AFFIRM:
Thank you for your constant support. I know that through thick and thin you are always with me. Never questioning, always loving.
Thank you for allowing me to become aware of your constant presence, support, and love.
Thank you for communicating to me your love and wisdom. I bathe in the sublime energy and light that I feel washing through me as you make your presence known.
Thank you for just being!

Getting Started

When you have read, contemplated and accepted the previous six steps, you can begin your work in opening up to the angelic realms. Always work with the method that you feel comes most naturally to you. No two people are the same, and so it is with the way in which you will communicate with your angels.

In order to help you to become a clear and open channel with the angelic realms it is important to pay some attention to your surroundings. Below are some suggestions for cleansing your home of any stale and negative energy that can hamper and confuse communication.

CLEANSING RITUAL

1. Clean, tidy, vacuum, and open all the windows so that your surroundings feel clean and fresh.

2. If possible, smudge your home using a sage smudge stick. This is a Native American tradition where the smoke from a smoldering herb stick is wafted around a room to purify the space.

3. Clap your hands in the corners of your rooms or sprinkle a little salt water to diffuse any negative energy residing there.

4. Burn some white candles. White represents purity.

5. If you have crystals, cleanse them in a solution of sea-salt. Some fragile crystals, such as moldavite, should be washed in fresh water rather than salt. If you do not have crystals at home, see page 50 for recommendations.

Making a Sacred Space

When you feel that you want to meditate or just be at one with your angels, it is very important to have a special place in your home where you know that you will feel at peace and will not be disturbed. By returning time and time again to the same place to communicate with your angels and guides, you will find that that area of the room takes on a different atmosphere. When your spiritual work is enacted in the same place, the resonance of that space changes as the atmosphere is repeatedly purified.

Your sacred space can be your sanctuary when you need a quiet place to meditate, contemplate, recharge your spirits, or just relax.

Certain tools enhance your communication with your angels. Gather together a selection of the following items, taking time to consider which appeal to you the most.

SCENT

Burning incense or aromatherapy oils is very helpful for relaxation, which is important if you are to be receptive to your angels. When choosing oils, go for those that naturally appeal to you. Calming oils include lavender, bergamot, geranium, and clary sage, but do bear in mind that these oils may not calm everyone. Likewise, basil is an excellent oil to burn when you need to keep focused (and wonderful for working at home in the evenings). However, some people may find it too stimulating for meditation work. Sweet orange will lift your spirits and help you keep balanced.

FLAMES

Burning candles help to still the mind and they are particularly useful for meditation. Candle color can also be used to transmit the nature of the contact you need with your angels: for friendship and purity choose white candles; for spirituality, purple candles; for healing, select blue candles; and for relationships – both romantic and platonic – choose pink. Always burn candles safely by securing them in candle-holders away from flammable items, and do not leave naked flames unattended for any period of time.

CRYSTALS

Crystals are energy transmitters. I always like to be surrounded by my favorite crystals, which can enhance spiritual energy while I work. If you are choosing crystals for the first time, you could select quartz, a powerful energy-amplifier, amethyst for healing and spirituality, or any that appeal to you.

COLOR

Color is a key stimulator for body and soul. You can introduce color into your space using favorite flowers and angel pictures. It is also a good place to keep angel affirmation cards (see page 54), if you have them.

MINI DISK

To practice meditations, keep a tape recorder or mini disk close to your altar. Choose the meditations or visualizations from this book that you wish to work with and record them in advance, playing them as you wish.

Ambience

Some people also like to play relaxing music when they meditate. You can choose soft, classical music, or any music with which you feel an affinity and calm, from Tibetan or Gregorian chants to dolphin song, South American pan pipes to love ballads. For others, music can act as an additional distraction rather than harmonious helper. For me, I feel that angelic energy is of a higher frequency and is more sensitive than music, so I prefer to communicate with my angels in the luxury of silence – but this is my personal choice. I am particularly fortunate in that I have been naturally able to open up as an angelic channel. Some of you may find that you can achieve this easily – all you have to do is enter your sacred space, take a moment to relax, and ask your angels to join you, whereupon you will be bathed with their energy, bypassing the need to meditate.

It can be helpful to practice connecting with angels when you are not in your sacred space. This technique can help you become less attached to your environment, and more attuned to your inner energy. Whenever you are about to begin a task – whether this is

EXERCISE TO INVITE ANGELS INTO YOUR HOME

1. Sit comfortably where you will not be disturbed, or in your sacred space.
2. Burn some candles, and place crystals and flowers around you if you wish.
3. Remove your shoes and place the soles of your feet flat on the ground.
4. Concentrate on your breathing to help you to relax.
5. Visualize roots growing downward from the soles of your feet into the earth below.
6. Feel the energy of the earth being drawn up into your body through the roots visualized in your feet.
7. Allow this energy to slowly permeate through every part of your body.
8. Once the energy has reached the crown of your head, visualize that it is now a white beam of energy linking you with the cosmos.
9. Through this beam of energy, invite your angels in to fill your home.
10. Feel them gather and enter your home and its environs, and feel their energy surround you.
11. When you are ready, thank them for coming and tell them that you will endeavor to keep the energy in your home pure.
12. Close yourself down by allowing the beam of light to dim and stop, and the energy of the earth to return through the roots in your feet to its source.

applying yourself to office work, making a telephone call, going into a meeting, or taking a drive in the car – relax and exhale slowly before you begin. Visualize your angels around you, protecting you in what you do that day. You can even add reminders to your diary before you start the day – list any decisions you need to make along with your appointments, and make a note to yourself to practice asking for guidance.

By performing this simple connecting ritual frequently before you embark on your everyday tasks, you are in effect creating a movable sacred space around you. You may find that this happens naturally the more you work within your designated sacred space.

A Sacred Space in Nature

For those of you who live in a temperate climate, it is wonderful to take some time to open up to your angels while being surrounded by nature. Standing or sitting outside while trying to relax and meditate may distract you at first, but persevere – it's worth it! You will eventually find that being at one with your angels in nature will make it easier for you to channel your angel's energies for healing on a planetary level.

Many people like to create their own sacred space in their garden. The elements of earth and air are already present, and if the sun is shining, fire is represented too. If you already have a water feature in your garden, on a sunny day you will have all four elements around you. Alternatively, you can place a small bowl of water near you as you meditate. The combination of the elements together enhances the energy surrounding you.

You can energize your outdoor sanctuary with flowers and herbs. Choose flowers instinctively, by the energy you sense through their colors. For herbal inspiration, plant sage for its cleansing properties, lavender to relax you, and rosemary to enhance mental clarity.

MEDITATION TO INVITE ANGELS INTO YOUR LIFE

1. Take yourself to a quiet place or to your sacred space (see page 49). Sit comfortably and relax. Remove your shoes, and place the soles of your feet flat on the floor.

2. Concentrate on your breathing. Inhale deeply, and feel the air fill every part of your lungs. Hold for a few seconds, then exhale.

3. Now as you inhale, imagine that you inhaling white light that is pure energy.

4. As you exhale, imagine that you are letting out a blue light of clutter, inhibitions, and blockages.

5. Continue practicing controlled breathing until you are feeling very relaxed.

6. Imagine that there are roots growing down from the soles of your feet through into the earth below.

7. Now feel the energy of the earth spread its way upward through these roots, through to your feet.

8. Feel it flow gradually through your feet, legs, torso, arms, and to your fingertips and beyond.

9. Now feel the energy rise through your throat to your head, and become aware of it reaching the "third eye" position, or the area between your eyebrows. Then feel the energy flow upward, to the crown of your head.

10. Invite your angels to fill you with their energies and to let you be aware of them. Take your time. Often, their vibrations will have to be adjusted to your personal frequency, but with practice this will happen more quickly and easily than at first.

11. Bathe and relax as the wonderful angelic energies fill every part of your being.

12. If you have questions or need guidance, now is the time to ask.

13. When you are ready, concentrate on your breathing again and be aware of the energy slowly diminishing from your body from head to toe, gradually draining from the soles of your feet back into the earth.

14. Thank your angels, and open your eyes.

Angel Affirmation Cards

Angel affirmation cards are a wonderful tool with which to engender an awareness of your angels and to help you to transform spiritually. If you don't have a pack of affirmation cards, you can use the Angel Messages in this book (which appear at the end of each section or chapter) or make your own Message Cards (see page 92) They act as a subtle mechanism to awaken your subconscious and align you with your soul and your angels.

Below are some suggestions for using affirmation cards and Angel Messages.

USING AFFIRMATIONS

1. Take one or more angel affirmation cards randomly from the pack, and meditate upon the message. To use the Angel Messages in this book., use the art of bibliomancy – close your eyes and flick through the book until you want to stop. Do this several times until you alight on an Angel Message page. Choose an affirmation or message that appeals to you, and contemplate on its personal message.

2. Use your affirmation cards daily as a quick way to attune to angelic guidance – before leaving to go to work, making a social engagement, or in the evening to help process the events of the day. Leave them in a bowl or in their box and randomly select a card and read its message for guidance. Alternatively, you can consciously choose a favorite affirmation for that day.

3. When you are feeling down and want some heavenly inspiration, just pick a card or choose an Angel Message to help lift your spirits.

4. When you need to send out healing thoughts to others, concentrate on an affirmation card or Angel Message to help you link with your angels, and then visualize sending out your healing thoughts through your angels.

Contacting Your Angels Through Dreams

One of the easiest ways to contact your angels is to ask them questions through dreams. This method of dream questioning was used by the earliest Kabbalists (followers of Kabbalah, the mystic system originating from Judaism).

Today this method is often called "dream incubation" by mystic practitioners.

While you are relaxing before sleep, consider your question and then affirm to yourself, either mentally or aloud:

Please my angels, enter my dreams so that I may learn to hear you. Please help me with (if you have a specific request). I also ask that you help me to remember clearly your message when I awake. Thank you.

If you have a specific question that you would like to ask your angels, meditate on it before you go to sleep. You may also like to write it down so that you can become more focused, and then slip it under your pillow. Do this if your question is very important, and keep a notebook and pen by the bed as you may find that you awake in the middle of the night with the answer, which you should then immediately write down before you go back to sleep.

As you drift off to sleep, meditate on the question and affirm either mentally or aloud:

Please my angels, help find the answer to my question which is (say your question) and help me remember your guidance clearly in the morning. Thank you.

Even if you are someone who does not usually remember their dreams, you may be surprised by this technique. This powerful affirmation causes a shift in your subconscious, so that your dreams will be more vivid and memorable than usual.

ANGEL MESSAGES

 You have reached the point in your life when you are ready and willing to reach out and grasp the hands of your angels - they have been waiting a long time for this to happen!

 Open up and let your angels and guides into your life.

 Feel your angels embrace you and surround you with unconditional love.

Free yourself of your past. Embrace the present and look forward to tomorrow.

 The angels will celebrate your triumphs, but will love you as easily for your failings.

 Place your trust in your angels and let them guide you through life.

 Once you have opened up the telephone lines between yourself and your angels – keep talking.

 Your guardian angel will never desert you. Let him fill your life with harmony, peace, and joy.

You are never alone. From the moment you were set upon this earth, your guardian angel has been your faithful and loving companion, trying to protect you from any pitfalls in your path.

Invite the angels into your life, and you will never be alone again.

Dowsing Your Affirmations

Many people enjoy dowsing for their affirmation or message for the day. You can either buy a pendulum or make one yourself. To make a pendulum, attach a crystal to a cord or a piece of personal jewelry, such as a ring. Make sure you wash the article first.

Hold the pendulum above the palm of your hand. Tune it in by asking it to show you which way represents "yes"; the most frequent response will be for the pendulum to swing clockwise. Then ask your pendulum to show you the direction for "no". This is often a straight line or the pendulum swings anti-clockwise. Carry out this simple exercise every time you use the pendulum. Now hold it above your affirmation cards, or page of Angel Messages in this book, and let your pendulum choose your affirmation. Many use this technique to ask a question and then dowse for the answer.

How Will You Know When Your Angels Are Connecting With You?

When angels enter your life, you will be aware of their pure, unconditional love and energy. As we are all so different, so are the ways in which the angels contact each and every one of us. Here are some of the ways in which angels make us aware of their presence in our lives.

Angel visions Many people today have witnessed angelic visions, at moments of stress or totally out of the blue. Anecdotal evidence indicates that these angels appear exactly as the seer had always imagined them to be, while others describe the many colors surrounding their angel.

Angel voices are sometimes heard clearly on a sound frequency, or they may be voices which come to you through telepathy. This is called clairaudience, which means "clear hearing". Remember that your angels want to protect and guide you, and that their voices will be consistently loving and enlightened. Therefore, if you think that you are hearing your angels but do not understand why the words are evil, then this has not emanated from your angels. If this becomes troublesome, always seek help from medical and spiritual professionals.

Clairsentience Many receive their angelic guidance as waves of energy that flow through the body. When I work with my angels and guides I usually feel waves of warm energy

flowing through the upper part of my body. They wash through me as waves upon waves.

I am very aware of being used as an open channel with the angelic and spiritual realms in my work. It does not matter if I am writing or if I am healing; within seconds, the appropriate energy flows through me. When I work on other people, I simply stand with my hand just above their shoulders and allow the energies to do their work. And many, many times people tell me that they feel hands working exactly where they are needed.

This form of channeling is called "clairsentience", or "clear feeling". When working with this form of communication, it is best to relax and realize that you must completely follow your intuition rather than apply logic to these sensations. Clairsentients also receive angelic interaction through their senses such as taste, touch, and smell. I often suddenly smell a fragrance which comes from nowhere, and I know that it is my guardian angel confirming his presence to me. However,

although I channel from the angelic realms and people come to me from far and wide for healing, I still sometimes question what am I feeling and doing – but I always hear my angels telling me to stop doubting myself. I try to stay right in the present, just letting the energies flow through me, as this is what I am meant to be doing.

Claircognizance Some people have the gift of "claircognizance", or "clear knowing", which means that they know something without knowing how. I found that when I began to read books on spiritual topics in order to expand my own knowledge, I found most of them surplus to my needs – but I had no idea how I had this knowledge!

Clairvoyance The word "clairvoyant" means "clear seeing", and many people testify that they receive their angelic communications through individual mental visual images, or a series of pictures. These images can sometimes be experienced as a photograph that suddenly appears in the mind, or they can take the form of a repetitive, slow-motion film showing people, events, symbols, or all of these.

One of my most intense clairvoyant experiences was when I was planning to visit a well-known personality in London. For two weeks before the appointment I kept seeing in my mind a picture of a simple, temple-like structure, jumping into my consciousness when I least expected it. Regardless of my previous experiences, I did begin to think that I was going crazy, and could simply not comprehend the meaning of this image, day in and day out – it was unchanging and there were no other clues in my mental pictures to its meaning, only this existed.

When I arrived at the appointed time at this person's house after two weeks, I was given my answer. There, standing prominently in their front garden, was exactly the building that I had been seeing in my visions.

Angel Encounters

There is an abundance of documented experiences and encounters with angels. Most people who actually see angels describe them as in paintings in a traditional style with either two or four wings. The sizes of the angels seem to vary a great deal, from very small to human-size, up to those whose angels are very tall. Many other people are aware of their angels appearing in a human form, appearing and disappearing as if from nowhere.

Other Ways of Knowing Your Angels Are With You

Many people find a mysterious white feather as confirmation that their angels are with them. I have never experienced this, but there are many signs of angelic presence to look out for:

* When conversing with your angels, you see dancing lights of energy.

* You hear a voice from nowhere.

* After a meditation when you have invoked your angels, you may feel a sensation around your body or against your hands, like a gentle electric current. If you then ask your angels to show that this is their energy that you are feeling, you may find that you can feel the tingling change in nature.

* As you are thinking about your angels, the atmosphere in the room changes to one of pure joy and love.

Synchronicity

The angels often use synchronicity and coincidence to get the message across to us that we are on the right path, and to make us aware of their presence. It is unbelievable how little nudges or interventions come at just the right time when we least expect them, and when they are most needed. Here's my latest experience of angelic timing.

I was sitting in our garden thinking about planning this book. It was a beautiful summer's day, and my thoughts turned to my asking my angels why, although I feel them and I know that they channel through me, I had never seen them or had a white feather left for me to find to affirm their presence.

I began to ask them to show me something tangible. Suddenly, within seconds, I heard the doorbell and there was a delivery of the most beautiful bouquet of large, white flowers for my daughter, Nicole, who was staying with us before her wedding.

As I took in the flowers I noticed that the label on the envelope simply stated "Angel Flowers". I was amazed by the synchronicity of the event; I knew that it was a sign that this book would be published, and that my angels were channeling through me.

Hearing Your Angels

Hark to the sound of heavenly choirs as they float through
a still summer's evening.

The sound of angels singing is a wonderful experience, and once heard is never forgotten. Unheard by most of us are the heavenly choirs that sing with joy every time we take a step forward in our journey toward spiritual enlightenment. They also celebrate those important dates in every soul's lifetime, such as their conception, birth, marriage, and parenthood.

The vibrations of your angels singing will also nurse you through illness and those times in your life when things are bad.

Your angels' singing can also have great meaning, especially when it is experienced in conjunction with a vision of a future apocalypse. Fred Astell told me of these unforgettable series of visions.

SOUND AND VISION

In Fred's first vision, he saw many battles going back to the beginning of time. It was very clear to him exactly what battles and time periods they were from by the armor and battle dress that was worn. This was then followed by a second vision of World War I and in the middle of this vision, the soldiers began singing.

Then Fred was given another vision where he was shown the countryside, but the sky was copper-colored and nothing was living. He felt very aware that he had been given a vision - the apocalypse that could be our future.

He sat up in bed awake, and in the corner of his room he saw a beautiful male angel who, in the sweetest tenor voice, sung a song that he repeated three times. Fred was told that the message was within the song, and that until we discover love in our hearts we will have nothing – we will destroy everything.

Fred knew that he had to track down this song. He finally found it in the BBC recording vaults and discovered that this song had been recorded three times – once each by Harry Secombe, John Hanson, and Nelson Eddy. The name of the song was "Ah, Sweet Mystery of Life".

The day after he told this wonderful story to his daughter, Chrissie Astell, I contacted her through a mutual friend to tell her that I was writing this book and was looking for angel experiences. I was under the impression that she merely had a passing interest in angels, and I was amazed to find out that not only did she run angel workshops, but the previous Saturday she had used my Angel Message cards for the first time.

ANGEL MESSAGES

 You will know when your angels contact you – you will be filled with joy love and happiness.

Relax and open up to the symphonies of angels.

 Let your angels in so that your days will be filled with harmony and joy.

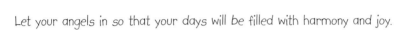

 Don't let the dark clouds gather in your mind – open yourself up to angelic love and harmony.

 Seize the moment and let your angels enter your life to help you to appreciate every day and waking moment.

 Once you have felt the loving warmth of your angels you will crave for it time and time again.

  Our angels contact us in many ways. Learn to open yourself up so that they can become more frequent.

In our darkest hours and our longest days our angels are yearning to comfort and protect us from all that life can throw at us.

  Everything happens for a reason – we must look beyond and understand why!

Your angels know everything about you – wouldn't you like to know something about them?

CHAPTER FOUR

Angels and the Stages of our Lives

At the point of conception, a new soul is shown its future by its guardian angel.

Angels and Conception

When a couple are having intercourse, the unseen soul of their future child is poised above them in the companionship of its guardian angel, who is assigned to guide the soul through its many journeys on earth.

The guardian angel shows this new soul what lays ahead – the lessons it will learn and what journeys it will travel during its forth-coming life cycle. Although we may be frightened of what the future holds, our guardian angel will reassure us that he will always be alongside us no matter what happens, but we must go through with our pre-ordained time on earth as part of our spiritual development.

As we develop in our mother's womb, our prenatal knowledge diminishes. The birthing

angels work alongside our Guardian Angel to help nourish our developing body and soul with love and protection.

The protection of a pregnant woman is fundamental to the angelic realms. She is carrying a new precious life, and therefore the physical incarnation of the soul's new point of entry into our world. She not only has the protection of her own guardian angel, but that of the unborn baby's guardian angel, plus a realm of angels known as "birthing angels." Their sole task is to guide a soul's entry into being.

Birthing angels communicate their love and goodwill to the mother to let her know how special she is during pregnancy. They spread their wings around her to protect her from accidents and disaster, and protect the baby she is carrying. During the birth, the birthing angels push and cajole the mother into taking things easier, even though she might try to

fight this physically. It is her birthing angels who help her to have a good night's sleep.

The birthing angels are very powerful as they have an extremely important double task in not only protecting a new soul's entry into this world but also they are looking after the well-being of the mother. The physical signs of their love can be seen by all. This is the time when people around notice how glowing and radiant the expectant mother is.

Once the baby is born, the angels will communicate guidance to you and also help you to protect your child from harm. This is where a mother's intuition comes from; when you know that if you do not do something immediately, your child could hurt itself, this knowledge comes from your angels. Angels are there to protect your child every second of his or her life, surrounding them always with gentle protection.

AN EXERCISE
DURING PREGNANCY

1. Take yourself to a quiet place where you will not be disturbed.

2. Sit in a comfortable chair or lie down on a bed if that is more comfortable. Close your eyes.

3. Concentrate on your breathing and become aware of inhaling and letting the air fill your lungs, and exhaling.

4. Breathe away all the tension in your body and imagine that you are surrounded with golden light.

5. Visualize a favorite place where you have felt at peace - a place in your garden, a childhood holiday memory, or simply imagine that you are floating in a scented bath.

When you are feeling relaxed, invite the birthing angels to gather around you and your unborn baby.

6. Invoke your angels to let you feel their love and protection. Ask them to let you feel their wings completely surrounding and cuddling you.

7. Stay as long as you wish with this feeling.

8. Thank your angels for their continued love and inspiration.

9. Open your eyes, stretch and go on your way or you may now wish to go into a peaceful slumber.

At the time of giving birth, you are surrounded by angels. You will have your guardian angel alongside you plus, if your partner is present theirs, plus the new baby's guardian angel and the birthing angels. All will help with the physical birth sending out their healing, protection, and love in abundance.

Angels and Childhood

When we are born our prenatal knowledge is mainly forgotten but children often retain a small iota of memory of their previous existence in the spiritual world. They also, often, still retain some memory of their past lifetimes in the physical world.

Often children, especially those who are lonely, play with what we call "invisible friends". They may be invisible to us but they are very real to those young who have not yet totally broken their ties with their spiritual origins and who still possess the ability to see the spiritual realms.

It is wonderful to converse with young children who tell you, without embarrassment, that they see and talk to their "friends" and their angels. If you meet any such children it is very good to encourage them to talk to you, as it is a truly wonderful experience. This is what happened with my daughter, Alexis, which demonstrates how young children still retain their links with the spirit world.

A CHILD'S VISION

We moved to Hampstead, London, six weeks after the birth of my youngest daughter, Alexis. We had bought this house from the children of the woman who had actually had it built in 1934, and the house was sold to us just after her death. We were told how she had loved to sit in the living room and look onto the golf course behind the garden. When she died, her ashes were scattered over her beloved golf course.

Often, I would see Alexis waving from the garden toward the house. When I asked her who she was waving to, she would tell me that an old lady was watching us, and that she was happy that her garden was still being enjoyed. Alexis related that she often saw this lady.

It is thought that a child's memories of the pre-natal spiritual worlds diminish over time. This is usually due to the strong vibrations from our planet that surround children, the energies from our earthly homes, and also due to the need to belong to their peer group. By this I mean that once children go into full-time education they can become programmed to think in a logical and numerate way and their natural, spiritual intuition can close down.

However, within many children a small, distant memory lingers about their guardian and birthing angels (see pages 16, 70). This is why so many children are able to reproduce such wonderful drawings and paintings of angels, even though they cannot remember actually ever seeing a picture of one.

It is human nature to worry about one's children, but after all worry is a negative vibration. Instead, regularly visualize loving energy protecting your children. With the following exercise you can also ask the angels and your child's guardian angel to link with your energies to protect your children.

EXERCISE TO ASK ANGELS TO WATCH OVER YOUR CHILDREN

1. Find a quiet place where you will not be disturbed. Sit down, relax, and close your eyes.
2. Concentrate on your breathing.
3. When you feel relaxed, visualize your child/children.
4. Now ask for your child or children's angels to share with you the parental love that you feel.
5. Ask the angels to watch over and protect your children from harm.
6. Invite the angels to share with you and your angels the love and harmony that they feel.
7. Invite the angels in so that you may receive and feel their response. Listen and feel this with your mind and your body. You may receive impressions of light, color or images - be open to these responses, and do not reject any feelings as being imaginary.
8. When these feelings fade, thank all the angels for sharing with you.
9. When you feel ready, open your eyes.

Angels and Teenagers

As most parents know and many of you I am sure remember, the teenage years are often filled with high levels of angst. This is a period when teenagers strive to conform rather than stand out from their friends and other peers. Great stress about personal appearance is often coupled with anxiety about academic performance, and scholastic achievement, or lack of, which may affect the adult years.

During this time our angels know that they will be excluded most consciously from our lives, so it is also a time when they will have to work their hardest. Teenagers may not like to discuss their belief in angels in case it makes them seem a little different from others. Teenage emotions can be topsy-turvy, swinging high and low at a moment's notice – or less. With the onset of puberty their love lives are open to experiment which may lead to great disappointment, and their need for friendship can often be rejected by those around them.

During this turbulent period, teenagers' guardian angels work overtime to help us through the good times and the bad times.

A VISUALIZATION TO HELP WITH TEENAGERS

1. Take yourself to a quiet place or your sacred space (see page 49), sit down comfortably and relax.
2. Concentrate on your breathing. Breathe in light and breathe out love until you feel ready to begin the visualization.
3. Ask your angels to link with your teenager's guardian angel to help protect and guide them.
Visualize them surrounding your teenager(s) with love and feelings of self-worth and confidence.
4. Ask them to make your child or children aware that whatever happens, you feel a deep and powerful love for them and that you will always be there for them.
5. Focus on this, and send out your own feelings of powerful love and energy to your child or children.
6. Thank your angels, and open your eyes.

Angels, Partnership, and Marriage

The marriage or partnership ceremony of two people who are truly in love is a wonderful occasion; realms of angels attend wishing love and joy upon the couple. The guardian angels of the partners or bride and groom and their families also add to the joyful energies which surround the happy couple.

The heavenly choirs sing in celebration of two soul mates having found each other and vowing to entwine their lives together. When commitment vows are exchanged, the contract is recorded in the Akashic record – this is the bank of ethereal memories and thoughts of all humankind.

When people are in love, their vibrational level shifts a little, naturally opening them up to letting their angels work closely with them. This is why when people are in love their whole demeanor appears to change. They seem to be filled with happiness and exhilaration, and will see their partner in the best light.

However, if the relationship starts to take a turn for the worse, you will notice that the atmosphere gets heavier as the natural open channel of communication with the angels begins to close down. But both of the couple's guardian angels will work very, very hard to make things better.

Angels in Adulthood

As adults, we have now reached the time when we should be able to make decisions about how we want to live our lives and what we want to strive for. We have reached a stage where we should start to realize that there is more to life than the daily grind of working from 9.00-6.00 and of pure materiality. This is a time where we begin to search for the true reasons for our life, opening ourselves up to the pure joy of spiritual awareness.

A CENTERING MEDITATION

1. Take yourself to a quiet place and either sit comfortably, or lay down.
2. Concentrate on your breathing. Inhale deeply and then exhale. Be aware of your lungs filling with air and then deflating.
3. Place your hands on your heart and feel your life force beating as it pumps blood around your body.
4. Become aware of the wonder of creation and how you are very much alive as you focus on your heart.
5. Visualize a white light in the center of your heart. Imagine this light expanding until it fills every part of your body.
6. Think that this is a spark of creative energy within you, and that you are an important part of the cosmos.
7. Take some time to feel what this means for you personally; you may feel a deeper sense of belonging.
8. When you are ready, concentrate on your breathing until you are ready to open your eyes.

Angels and Death

Angels frequently appear to those who are dying in order to help them make their transition from this world to the other side easier. A lady I met told me the following:

A FINAL VISION

My mother, it has to be said, was an extremely difficult and unhappy person. When we gathered around her death bed, a radiant smile illuminated her whole face. I must admit that this was probably the happiest I can remember her looking for many years. She was looking into the corner of the room and her gaze stayed there; it was obvious she was looking at something that was making her very, very happy. As a Christian I am completely convinced that she saw her guardian angel who had come to help ease her transition over to the other side.

When my aunt was dying, I was there every day with my parents as she slipped into semi-consciousness. During the last two days there were many times when she was lucidly talking to all of her sisters and brothers who had died before her as if they were alive, and were helping her to make her dying easier. On the last day I believed that she also talked with her angels whom she could see, and who were gently easing her through her transition from this world and into the next.

When my father was dying, it was similar to the experience of my mother. He also slipped into a semi-conscious state which lasted about a week. During the times that he was lucid, he also spent much of it talking to his dead brothers and sisters who were waiting for him on the other side. During his last night, he also looked radiantly happy when gazing toward one part of the room. I knew then that his angels had come to take him away, and that he would not live another day.

CHAPTER FIVE

When Angels Can Help Us

When you feel totally alone with your troubles,
remember that once your angels enter your life you will be
surrounded by love, peace, energy, and joy!
And they are always willing to lend a helping hand.

No matter how confident we seem to the outside world, this is often a facade masking an inner need for security and assurance. In order to communicate fully with our angels, it is important to work on ourselves in order to acknowledge and embrace who we truly are.

To achieve a heightened state of consciousness, we must first learn to embrace what Carl Jung called our shadow. This part of our personality encompasses those hidden, negative aspects that we do not like to admit to. However, it is the balance of both our positive and negative attributes that makes us the people we are. The acknowledgement of our shortcomings, such as lies, envy, criticism, and self-pity brings the self-knowledge that changes our perspective on life.

Many people go through a lonely and painful journey which many called "the Dark Night of the Soul" (see page 18). This is often caused by an extremely stressful experience, the pain of which forces us to take a long hard look at ourselves and everything around us. As we emerge from this stage we find that we have actually uncovered core truths that will transform our experience into a period of self-healing and renewal. By changing our darkness into light, we reconnect with our soul and face our shadows.

If you have difficulty accepting your "dark shadow", it could be due to an underlying belief that only the perfect deserve to be loved and are worthy of angelic communication. Nothing could be further from the truth. Our angels love us completely and unconditionally. It is, however, very beneficial to learn to love ourselves, progress and live life to the full. The following exercise will help.

EXERCISE FOR
SELF-ACCEPTANCE

Go to a quiet place or your sacred space (see page 49) and sit comfortably. Remove your shoes and place the soles of your feet flat on the floor. Close your eyes and concentrate on your breathing, inhaling deeply, then exhaling. When you feel relaxed, you are ready to begin.

1. Visualize that there are roots growing down from the soles of your feet burrowing deep into the earth below – no matter how many floors up you are.

2. Now imagine that through these roots the energy of the earth is being drawn up into your feet and then further up into your legs, then through your torso.

3. Feel the energy flow through your arms, hands, and fingers, through your heart and throat, up to your head and then through the crown of your head.

4. As you inhale, visualize that you are breathing in the life-energy of the universe and within this will be everything you need for the new you – love, health, vitality, joy, and a new way of perceiving the world.

5. When you exhale, imagine that you are expelling everything that you don't want or don't need – the negative energy that is blocking and hindering you. Expel with every out-breath any dark thoughts, such as anger or jealousy.

6. Think: the time has come for you to release your old ways of living and thinking.

7. Now ask your angels to help you to achieve this makeover and to enter your life.

8. Take some time feeling your angels surrounding you with their love, radiance, and guidance. Feel their energy as it enters your body as swirls of heat and/or pulsating currents.

9. Allow yourself to wallow in the wonderful vibes that your angels are feeding every part of your being.

10. When you are ready to finish, concentrate on your breathing as the energy of the universe slowly drains from your body back down through the roots of your feet and into the earth below.

11. Thank your angels, open your eyes, and move on with your life.

Improving Your Relationships

Your angels are very happy to work with you to help you to create or improve your relationships with other people. Your own guardian angel and that of the other person, or people, are involved in this process.

In every relationship there are the good times, but there can also be troublesome times when constant conflict or problems hinder communication between you. These situations arise to help you heal old issues, and then to grow and develop. We learn our patterns of relationships from our parents (which may or may not be a good thing), but it is our respon-

sibility to take a step back from a relationship and understand what is going wrong, rather than blame the other party. This gives us a chance not just to rescue the relationship but also to remedy our own attitudes and feelings.

Inviting our angels to help and guide us in these circumstances will help to expand our capability to experience a truly happy and meaningful communication. If there are problems, we can ask our angels to contact the angels of the other person involved, and this can often smooth the way to a peaceful and happy reconciliation.

EXERCISE TO AID RELATIONSHIPS

1. Take yourself to a quiet place and sit comfortably. Relax, and concentrate on your breathing.

2. Invite your guardian angel to come and help you and explain how you feel.

3. Visualize the other person in the equation and their guardian angel.

4. Next, ask your guardian angel to make contact with this other person's guardian angel.

5. Become aware of the connection between the two angels. Feel the energy difference between your guardian angel and that of the other person's.

6. Just as you converse with your personal angel, now visualize that you are opening up to communicate with both of the angels, and explain how you feel and how you would like them to help you.

7. Ask your questions, and be receptive to any words that may come through to you.

8. Know that this connection will make a difference to your relationship.

9. When you are ready, thank both of the guardian angels. Become aware of your breathing and, when you are ready, open your eyes.

Cutting the Cords That Bind Us

We become attached to many things throughout our lives. Painful memories often influence our behavior, and we can also become tied invisibly to our jobs and possessions.

When you are in a loving relationship, an invisible cord binds you and your partner. Similarly, if you are involved in an unhappy relationship you are also invisibly bound, and often find it difficult to break free. The powerful archangel Michael (see opposite, and pages 11–12) personifies strength and protection on a physical and spiritual level. He is usually depicted with a cloak of cobalt blue and a mighty sword. It is upon Michael that we call if we wish to cut these ties, especially in situations of rejection and hurt.

EXERCISE TO CUT TIES FROM THE PAST

1. Take yourself to a quiet place, sit comfortably, and relax.
2. Concentrate on your breathing.
3. Focus on what, or whom, you wish to be released from.
4. Become mindful of how you are bound to it or them.
5. Invite the archangel Michael into your life to cut the link and dissolve the cords completely. Ask Michael, from your heart, to help you in love and light, and visualize Michael holding his sword, then cutting the cord that binds you.
6. See in your mind's eye the cord being cut and then dissolving. Do not be surprised if you experience this momentarily as a feeling in your body.
7. Ask Michael to give you the strength and spiritual protection to help you overcome your problems so that you can grow physically and spiritually.
8. Inhale the energy of the universe and the love of your angels.
9. When you are ready, thank Michael and your angels for their help.
10. Open your eyes.

How Angels Can Help Heal a Broken Heart

We all go through situations in life in which we think that our heart is broken and feel at the end of our tether. It could be through a great personal disaster, or because a personal relationship has gone wrong.

Our heart is vital not only to our physical health, but it is also essential for our mental, emotional, and spiritual well-being. It is from our heart that feelings of depression, loneliness, anger, and hurt stem.

When we open up our hearts to let in our angels, we can work to amplify our capacity for love, spirituality, compassion, and giving. They will also help us to heal our emotional centers, to mend a broken heart and to develop love for ourselves and for others.

EXERCISE TO CLEANSE AND HEAL YOUR HEART

1. Lie down comfortably in a quiet place. Close your eyes.

2. Concentrate on your breathing. As you inhale, feel your body fill with air and as you exhale, feel the tension being released and expelled from your body.

3. When you are ready, sense the power of your heart. Place your hands on it and feel it pumping your life blood throughout your body.

4. Now become aware of its outer casing. Does it feel healthy, or do you sense that it is damaged in any way?

5. Become aware of the inside of your heart. Is it full of trauma and wounds, or is it full of love?

6. Invite your angels to come in and heal it. Ask them to allow you to become aware of their presence. Become aware of your angels filling your heart with a bright, white warm ray of light which will heal and mend it.

7. Feel your heart expand as it receives this gift from your angels.

8. Feel the outer walls of your heart healing, and become aware of the white energy filling every inner cavity with a warm and loving energy.

9. This angelic energy will soothe your old wounds as you feel your old hurts and anger slowly dissipate, to be replaced by love and compassion. Forgive and free yourself from any guilt or pain that you have been holding on to.

10. Relax and be open to all that is happening. Now, if you wish, think if there is anyone to whom you want to send this energy in order to forgive them or to heal them. If so, visualize a bridge of light from your heart to theirs, from which flows your forgiveness.

11. Now visualize a ray of white light emanating from your heart center through your entire body and beyond, until you feel cocooned in a warm heat and energy that fills you completely.

12. Feel yourself being gently washed by a warm, white energy generated by your angels who are also caressing you with their love and goodwill.

13. Thank your angels. Concentrate on your breathing again; open your eyes.

Letting Go of the Past to Find Peace in the Present

Most of us find it difficult to forget past hurts and not allow them to influence us. It could be that our achievements were never good enough for our parents, or that we can't let go of negative comments made by some of our peer group. We may have suffered a slight at work, or were rejected by someone to whom we were attracted romantically. Equally, we could be harboring old feelings of hatred against someone who has gone out of their way to cause us

or our family pain or sorrow. Although these negative influences in our lives are quite common, they are certainly not healthy. If they are allowed to fester within our minds for a prolonged period, they may lead to depression and even physical illness.

You can invite your angels to help remove this negativity from your life and instead teach you how to feel positive and at peace with yourself. Try the exercise opposite.

EXERCISE TO HELP YOU TO LET GO OF THE PAST

1. Go to a quiet place or your sacred space (see page 49) where you will not be disturbed.

2. Close your eyes and concentrate on your breathing until you feel relaxed.

3. As you inhale deeply, visualize that you are breathing in a pure, white light. As you exhale, visualize that you are breathing out all the stale, negative energies that are stored up within you.

4. Now visualize that the white light that you are breathing in is starting to fill your whole body.

5. Visualize that you are going up five steps and through an open doorway into a beautiful meadow filled with flowers. The sky is cornflower blue; you can hear the birds singing and the buzzing of insects.

6. Walk through this field until you come to a pure stream, which is running into a pool of warm, clear blue water.

7. There are some steps down into this pool. You follow them and enter the warm water.

8. See your angel, who appears before you to help you into the pool and wash you. As you wash in this warm water, feel that your angel is helping you to wash away all your negative energies and thoughts.

9. Feel them dissolve in the water.

10. Now, as your angel holds your hand and leads you back up the steps, feel the harmony and peace that is radiating from him surround your body and dry you like a warm wind.

11. Feel your whole body and mind fill with love, compassion, and peace.

12. When you are ready, wave goodbye to your angelic companion, and thank him.

13. Walk back through the meadow, through the open doorway. and back down the five steps.

14. Concentrate on your breathing again and, when you are ready, open your eyes.

What We Can Learn From Angels

Through reading this book I hope that you will feel that, although our life can be a very solitary journey, you can be secure that your angels will always love you, no matter how far you stray from our chosen pathway.

Death should not be feared as it is just a part of the process of our evolvement as spiritual beings; our angels will always be there holding our hands when we are afraid of the unknown, helping to guide toward the next chapter of our existence.

Angels have much to teach us including compassion, tolerance, awareness, and wisdom. By opening up to our angels we learn how to spiritually evolve beyond our mundane physical existence to a greater knowledge and understanding which will bring us one step nearer to our Creator.

Angels teach us to trust our intuition, and to realize that some things are worth waiting for. Tied up with this is patience. We must trust that when the time is right a new door will open, a new opportunity will arise, and our next step along our pre-ordained pathway will be made clear to us.

We must always remember that, in the spirit of eternal truth, an ending always indicates a new beginning, and we must trust that our angels will always help us through any kind of adversity that we encounter. With loving patience and care they will gently guide us through to the next stage of our lives, even if we feel downhearted and depressed. They will try to lift our spirits and show us that in order to become better human beings we have many lessons to learn, and not everything turns out for the best. As a result of angelic guidance, however, we can look beyond difficulties so that we can move on to the next stage of our lives.

By asking our angels for help and inviting them into our lives we not only open ourselves up to their energies which will surround and feed us with love, hope, happiness, and tolerance, but by so doing we benefit the whole of humankind.

ANGEL MESSAGES

Some doors may close to me, but I know that others will always be open.

When I invite my angels to gather around me I know that the whole of mankind will benefit.

Patience I have not, but my angels have it in abundance.

The presence of my angels has blessed my life in ways that I could never have foreseen.

I invite my angels to help me to let go of the past so that I can have peace in the present.

I place my trust in my angels to help me to make the best of this life.

Not a day passes when I do not feel the love, happiness, and compassion of my angels.

My angels fill me with the energy and light of the universe.

Knowing my angels has completely changed the way I see the world around me.

Many a time I feel heavy with despair, but as soon as my angels surround me with their sublime energy, the load lightens and then fades away.

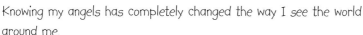

Making Your Own Angel Affirmation Cards

If you are not able to purchase angel affirmation cards, or if you would prefer to make your own, start by photocopying the Angel Message pages in this book. Cut out the Messages and stick them onto thick card. You could decorate the reverse of each with your own design – let each Message inspire an individual image that is personal to you. Make a minimum of 28 cards (to represent four weeks, or 28 days). 52 cards work well, as you will have one card for each week of the year.

When your communicative abilities with your angels become more developed, and you are conversing clearly, keep a note of the messages you receive. Gradually, build up a store of personal messages and use them on your cards. Keep your cards in a bowl or basket, ready for you to choose at any given moment.

Angel Websites

www.angellight.co.uk
New site; includes angel stories and details on angel workshops.

www.angelrealm.com
True stories of angel encounters.

www.angelsmag.com
Online magazine devoted to all things angelic, including discussion forum and contributors' angel experiences.

www.applecity.com/Angels
Features include "True Angel Stories", readers' poems, and angels Q & A.

http://kimbasangels.com/spirit.html
Angel biographies, the hierarchy explained, angel art gallery.

www.mcsi.net/alahoy/angels.htm
Channeled messages from angels Michael, Uriel, Gabriel et al.

http://paranormal.about.com/msub2.htm?once=true&
More angelic encounters in Angels & Demons section of paranormal phenomena site.

www.spirithome.com/angels.html
Personal site devoted to faith and spirituality.

www.spiritual-endeavors.org/channeling/angels-help.htm
How angels can help you; angel Michael as channeled through Diandra.

http://theinnervoice.com
Online angel 'zine includes prayers, affirmations, and evidence of angels.

Newsgroup:
alt.religion.angels

About the Author

Vanessa Lampert is the author of the *bestselling guide and angel affirmation pack*, *Angel Messages* (Cico Books, 2001). She is a clairvoyant and healer who inherited her gifts from her father. She is also a *successful businesswoman*, who ran the Enigma chain of gift stores in London, which specialized in New Age products. Like *Angel Messages*, which include divine messages channeled by Vanessa, *Angel Voices* is also the result of her special relationship with her own angels and her unique clairvoyant abilities.
Vanessa lives in London, UK, and is married with three daughters.

By the same author:

Angel Messages (Cico Books, 2001)
Practical Kabbalah For Magic and Protection (Cico Books, 2002)

Acknowledgments

I would like to thank my husband, Jeffrey, my three daughters Nicole, Simone, and Alexis, and my mother, Lily Pepper, for their continued love and support. Thanks, too, to my agent Chelsey Fox for her advice and guidance, and to everyone at Cico Books, especially Cindy Richards, Liz Dean – for being a wonderful and inspiring editor – and to Jacqui Mair for her beautiful illustrations. I am also grateful to Chrissie Astell of Angellight.co.uk and to Lauren of angelfire.com for their contributions.

And a special big thank you to my angels for their assistance in writing this book by guiding my every step with wisdom and love.

I would love to hear about your angel stories and experiences. If you would like them to be included in future books, please submit them by post to: Vanessa Lampert, c/o Cico Books, 32 Great Sutton Street, London EC1V 0NB, or email them to vanessalampert@aol.com. Please let me have, in writing, your permission to publish your story, and say if you would like your name to appear, or if you would prefer to remain anonymous.